Effective Multitasking

7 Habits to Boost Your Effectiveness

PIOTR NABIELEC

Effective Multitasking

Copyright © 2013 by Piotr Nabielec

Cover art by Mikolaj Walanus (www.walanus.com)
Illustrations by Mikolaj Walanus (www.walanus.com)
Edited by Abraham Storer

ISBN: 978-83-937607-0-1

This title is also available as an ebook product.
www.EffectiveMultitasking.com
E-mail: info@effectivemultitasking.com

Table of Contents

Preface

We live in busy times. Our task lists and responsibilities are constantly growing. Effectiveness is key. Doing two or more things at the same time proves ineffective. True multitasking is a myth - no one should expect it to work. However, it is possible to deal with our e-mail, events, and tasks in a manner that appears simultaneous from the perspective of hours and days. This is what I call "effective multitasking."

I studied and discussed productivity habits and techniques for more than 10 years and found that most people, regardless of their company and position, are struggling to keep up with their e-mail, task lists, and calendars. A highly skilled professional with over 20 years of experience in the IT industry once told me that he approached each day with a clear picture of tasks to accomplish, but during the course of the day something magical happened where incoming e-mails, phone calls, and discussions derailed him so that he rarely accomplished half of what he originally planned. That meant overtime, stress, and the loss of precious time.

While sharing productivity habits with other co-workers, one eventually shouted with enthusiasm that these simple habits are so important that they should be taught at schools! That event inspired me to write this book. I believe simple habits can radically change productivity levels and that the key is clarity. We can get a few steps closer to "effective multitasking."

While writing this book I learned a lot from people that were reviewing this material and I hope their input made the content and the examples clearer. They also gave me faith that this really can help many people. This book would not be what it is without a few people that I would like to give special thanks and praise. Aga who is the love of my life, for her patience, openness to discussion, and helpful hints. Dominik Gazda for his continuous support, open mind and being with me from the very first lines of this book. Mikolaj Walanus for his inspiring graphic work - the cover, all the illustrations, and web page creation. Abraham Storer for his patience and conscientiousness while doing so many corrections to this text. Sebastian Bigos for the inspiring conversations that provided the spark to actually start writing. Tomasz Kaczanowski for his valuable hints. My family for being with me no matter what. God for his grace and all the gifts and talented people that have surrounded me my whole life.

I would also like to thank all the early reviewers of this book: Sandi Mitchell, Eoin McCoy, Dominik Gazda, Piotr Kuchta, Krzysztof Raś, Uttam Sarkar and Henryk Metz.

Introduction

Have you ever experienced a situation like this: you come to work, make a good plan for the day, and a few hours later come to realize that you responded to a number of e-mails and pressing issues, but made no progress on the tasks planned for that day?

We have e-mails. We have meetings. At work, every hour brings changes like a rotating kaleidoscope. Urgent tasks, important e-mails, and professional distractions make us feel like we have lost control, as chaos filtering from different channels bombards our minds. How do we cope with this?

Many of us struggle to respond to incoming e-mails in a timely manner or prioritize tasks across different projects. Suddenly many things left for the future become urgent and important and there are days that we must completely switch into fire-fighter mode.

At times such as this, you may consider that there has to be a better way to organize your work, improve productivity and accomplish more in a limited amount of time. If you know this feeling, simple techniques contained in this book will help you organize, relax, engage fully and become a reliable person. This book will help you find your natural style of organization and put it into practice.

My story

There are several events in my life that completely changed the way I think and operate. One of them happened a few years ago when I had a helpful conversation with my colleagues at work about running. They were attending marathons while I struggled to run for five kilometers without dying. Every time I finished a run, I had to lie on my bed for half an hour. Still, I was able to run like this for four consecutive years. After talking to them and reading just a few chapters from a book they recommended, I could run for more than five kilometers with no additional training and immediately after coming back home I was able to operate normally. I even felt much better after the run than I felt before!

For several years before that conversation, I had good motivation and sincere resolution; I put my whole heart into my efforts. However, my efforts were completely foolish. With just a few changes to my running habits, I was able to double my four-year progress within the next six months. Until that moment I believed that good motivation, sincere resolution and whole-hearted effort were enough in everything I did. Now I know it is not.

At that time I determined to do things more wisely. If I wanted to be effective at my work, in my personal life, or even running, I knew I needed to know the appropriate techniques and rules, so that I would not waste time. I started to study habits that productive people have, putting them into practice and then sharing them with my colleagues and friends.

I noticed obvious results in those who followed these habits - simple techniques changed the way they worked as they were able to see the big picture and prioritize tasks more easily. Most importantly, they didn't have to memorize everything. This helped to minimize their stress so that they could engage fully and creatively in daily tasks without the fear that something would be lost.

This book shares techniques that may offer a revolution or a small improvement to you. I hope this will have an effect on you similar to the few, wise pieces of advice I received about running some time ago.

Inspiration

There are tons of books and articles to boost your effectiveness. Usually they are very good, but the problem is they mostly work for people that are organizational geeks and may be inaccessible to the rest of us struggling to catch up with daily tasks at work and at home. You can read "Getting Things Done" or "Zen to Done," "The Seven Habits of Highly Effective People," "Kanban," "Scrum," "Flow," "Pomodoro Technique" and many more. But you need something really simple, right?

The objective is to make a simple system that will be visual, easy to learn, and help you organize at work. At the same time, it should allow you to focus on your tasks, not on the system. I hope you will find such a system through this book and that it will help you achieve success.

Habits

The key to success is to form a way of behavior that will work for you, even if you don't actively think about it. It is not merely about self-control. It is about taking one step at a time and forming a habit that is completely unconscious.

Do you know how long it takes to form a habit? Imagine you want to start drinking a daily glass of water or do fifty sit-ups before breakfast. How long will it take to perform automatically, without self-control? A great article on PsyBlog, "How Long to Form a Habit?", answers that question with a simple number - 66 days on average. It reveals the very simple truth that it will take you two months of daily repetition before a behavior becomes a habit. Give yourself time and just be regular. Do not give up too early!

Have you ever noticed that some people who have their houses close to the airport can completely ignore even the loudest aircraft? On the other hand, some can recognize their favorite songs just after the first few notes. You may have recognized this phenomenon when conversing with someone in a noisy environment. When you focus, it nearly seems that the rest of the world does not exist. How is it possible that some people ignore big disruptions while others seem to be tuned into something subtle? It is all about giving positive and negative responses to our impressions. If you practice ignoring something you will slowly become less sensitized. If you give positive, practical responses to your impressions, your sensitivity will increase.

In this book, we will be working on building the right habits with practical, positive responses.

IT WILL TAKE YOU TWO MONTHS OF DAILY REPETITION
BEFORE THE BEHAVIOR BECOMES A HABIT

What is it?

We will work on building effective habits using systems that are visual and easy to remember. The key is to practice regularly. You will learn how to manage your e-mail inbox, calendar, and task list. The heart of this system is based on a mind map, which stores all important information in one place, using a visual format that displays information, while preserving a hierarchy of priorities. Along with the mind map, it's wise to use color-coded formats whenever possible so that both hemispheres are fully engaged in the process.

This system works perfectly at work, but can also be used at home to organize daily tasks. The mind map system performs ideally in the workplace environment because of the consistent availability of your computer, phone, and colleagues. If you find it working for you in your professional environment, you should be able to use it at home, or wherever you have access to a PC or a tablet.

How to read this book

This rather short book focuses on seven practical habits. You will have to practice these habits and adjust them for your work environment and personal style. Just reading the book won't change anything. I strongly suggest reading the whole book, while identifying which habits will give you the most progress and will be easiest to learn in the beginning. When you are ready, read identified chapters once a day for several consecutive days and keep practicing! When you finish the book and still have no idea where to begin, there is a chapter waiting to help you take the first steps.

Each habit contains a description, summary, and most importantly, examples that will help you put the theory into practice. Be sure that you fully understand and appreciate each habit-driven behavior. They are intended to help you organize! The most important aspect is patience – put the habits into practice one by one. As mentioned earlier, it will take several months to do it naturally. Expect great gains!

Habits are numbered, but it does not mean that you cannot proceed to the next one before the previous is fully formed. Trust your intuition, because while reading the book you will immediately realize which habits are most relevant to you.

Are you ready?

Let us start!

Inbox as a Task List

Let's assume, on average, you receive somewhere between 10 and 100 e-mails a day. That makes thousands of e-mails a year. How do you navigate through them effectively and at the same time lose none of the important messages?

We will turn your e-mail inbox into a task list. Most of the time, it will be nearly empty. Navigating through it and searching for important pieces of information will take you seconds. There are just four habits that will do it for you.

Habit 1: Classify action

The first and most important habit involves quickly and intuitively responding to each e-mail with two very important questions.

1. Does it require any action from me?

Look at the e-mail. Does it really need you to act? Do you need to read the whole message? If it is short, just read it and classify. If it is long and you need more time to read it, this is a potential task for a future time.

We would like to convert your inbox into a task list, so it should contain only messages that require an action from you, such as reading the whole message, understanding the details, responding, thinking about the solution etc.

Think about it for a moment: if it is in your inbox, it requires an action from you.

IF IT IS IN YOUR INBOX,
IT REQUIRES AN ACTION FROM YOU

---

2. Will I ever need this?

If your e-mail does not require an action from you, it can either be useful material for another day or it is garbage. The problem most people face is that they have a fear of the 'Delete' icon and they do not know the meaning of this simple button on their keyboards.

When it is garbage, such that you know you will never need to read it again, be brave and click 'delete' – Voila! Your time and disk space are saved.

This is it: it requires an action from me OR it is material for future reference OR it is garbage. It will take some time for this simple classification to become completely unconscious for you.

Take your time to process the main folder of your inbox right now. Just start. Try to process a hundred messages a day and split the whole process into several days. This way the habit will form more quickly. Remember it may take two months or more to form! The next habit will help you organize your folders for storing e-mails.

IT REQUIRES AN ACTION FROM ME

OR

IT IS MATERIAL FOR FUTURE REFERENCE

OR

IT IS GARBAGE

Visualization

You always have breaks while reading your e-mail. When you look at your inbox after a period of time, it may contain a large number of unread items left to classify. There is a very quick action you can do to easily pick the most important messages first. How do you do this? Let us use visualization.

Usually the most important messages, that will likely require your action, are sent directly to you or to you and your colleagues. For the less important, you are probably on the CC line. One may use Microsoft Outlook or another e-mail service to automatically apply colors to such messages.

Example how to set colors for Microsoft Outlook

Go to View > Settings

Click "Conditional Formatting" or "Automatic Formatting" button

You should now be able to add two rules.
- Let's call them "To me only" and "To me and others."
- For the first, chose the red font and for the condition mark "Where I am" and "the only person on the To line."
- For the second – blue font and "Where I am" – "on the To line with other people."
(Of course you may use different fonts and colors. This is just a proposal).

When you apply these settings, some messages will change their colors and immediately catch your attention. These are good candidates to classify first as they are very likely to demand an action from you.

Other techniques

Why keep your inbox nearly empty?

Some people use flags or other techniques available to identify items that require action. However, the main problem is that our brain is not a CPU. The logical flow of information is only a small part of what we perceive as important. We have emotions, impressions, and memory. Both hemispheres process this information, performing the analysis from different angles.

When your inbox functions as a task list, it provides a clear visual signal of how much work is left. It can be summarized with just a simple look. You may think, "not much" or "ouch, too many, I need to start delegating or do something about it." The task list satisfies the logical part of your brain, while also providing an important, immediate impression.

Examples

You are reading an e-mail from one of your team leaders and after the second sentence you realize it is just for your information, but has nothing to do with you and you do not even need to read the whole message. You immediately stop reading at this point and drag it to one of the folders for future reference. One day it may be important to come back to this message.

You are reading a company announcement about a colleague's promotion with a list of his new responsibilities. You realize you will never need this information again and bravely delete this!

Another company announcement contains a few names that may be useful in the future, but not necessarily now, so without reading the whole message you move it to one of the folders.

There is a message automatically sent by one of the system tools and informs you about a status change of something unimportant. Another time you bravely delete it.

You see a long message from your boss to you and a few other colleagues (probably colored blue by Outlook). It is important for you to read this; however, it is not urgent. You simply leave it in your inbox as a task for a moment when you have more time. It can be now, but it can be later if you have other things to do.

There is a short message from your boss (probably colored in red by Outlook) with a simple question. Since this is urgent, you should immediately act – respond to the e-mail and immediately after clicking 'send,' drag it to one of the folders for future reference.

You received an announcement from the IT department saying that in a week, on Monday at 3PM, there will be a planned network downtime. They are very sorry, but they need to do it. It will last for just half an hour. This may be a very important half hour! You create a half-hour calendar event for Monday at 3PM named "Network downtime." Next, you drag the email into the event you created, save it and also drag the original email into one of the folders. When a reminder pops up the next Monday, you know 15 minutes in advance that you should re-plan your work, so that for the next thirty minutes the network connection will not be required. No surprises, no worries.

The message you read asks you to complete the company survey. The deadline is in two weeks and you currently do not have time to do it, but you would like to give your opinion. You leave it in your inbox as a task and at the same time put an event in your calendar for the final date to submit the survey. You may give it a name, such as "Survey deadline," and drag the original message into the content of the event. Setting a reminder for a day or two before the deadline is probably important. Leaving the email in your inbox makes this a task for you and the calendar event will ensure that you don't miss the deadline.

Summary

This habit does not require much effort and provides some quick improvements. You may process a hundred messages in just a few minutes. Delete garbage, move most of the messages to folders for saved material, and leave just a few of them which require your attention and action. You do not answer all of them immediately, and do not need to read them all. First classify the emails and determine your tasks. Then you can plan accordingly. When you start doing this, you will quickly realize how many e-mails received do not require any action from you and only blur the picture of tasks to perform.

Habit 2: Storing materials

Subfolders

How many times have you searched for something for a really long time saying, "I had it somewhere?" Or perhaps you have asked your colleague to send a message once again - now another person must find the message because you couldn't.

This is a very common problem. Quick access to important pieces of information is crucial for personal effectiveness. Otherwise confusion sidetracks your thought process. It may take several minutes to come back to the focus you had before.

To effectively store information in your inbox we will use folders and learn how to quickly search them. The rule of thumb is very simple: messages of the same type should reside in the same folder. The main problem is categorization. Two of the most common mistakes involve having no folders at all or having too many of them. With no folders, or actually one big folder, it is like having only one huge wardrobe in the whole house filled with clothes, books, dishes, and cosmetics. This does not sound normal! On the other hand, having twenty is also impractical, because you need to remember where you put things. The best classification happens when you do it spontaneously, without much thinking.

I strongly suggest having no more than seven to ten sub-folders, for example:

- Universal – static content - login details, key presentations, key project structures, etc.
- Sent by Automated Tools – usually from different IT systems – important ones
- Personal – non-work related sent among your colleagues
- Your current projects

You can do a very quick exercise to understand why you shouldn't have too many folders. Put one hundred random messages in your folder, start your timer, and move all the emails to the correct folders. When you finish classification, stop the timer and write down the time. Try doing this with five, ten, twenty, or more folders and you will immediately notice the difference.

You may ask why people create so many folders. Often we think that many folders will help us when we want to find specific pieces of information. It is exactly like the books on our shelves at home. We keep similar books together, but there are so many categories! Working with computers, we have the advantage of a very quick search mechanism. Instead of creating multiple folders we need to learn how to search effectively.

Search

One day I realized that most people do not know how to use e-mail search engines! In Outlook and Gmail we usually use single words as the search criteria or even worse, we use two words thinking that it will find messages that contain both words, rather than either of them. Actually, these engines are far more powerful.

For Outlook I strongly suggest googling "Learn to narrow your search criteria for better searches in Outlook." For Gmail I suggest googling "Gmail Advanced Search."

How to find messages in Outlook in a very short time
(Gmail is very similar, actually):

E-mails from Andrew received last week
    from: Andrew received: last week

E-mails with attachment, received this week
    received: this week hasattachment: yes

E-mails with both "Project" and "Next steps" in their subject, body, or attachments
    Project AND "Next steps"

E-mails sent to both Andrew and David
    to: Andrew to: David

E-mails with "Connect" in the subject and "Meeting minutes" in subject, body, or attachments
    subject: Connect "Meeting Minutes"

With just a little practice, searches will become far more efficient than going to a folder, sorting by column, and trying to locate the right message.

Examples

You open your inbox and realize that you have several folders with names of people you work with, including your boss. Rather than sifting through many folders, the search tool can find these messages more efficiently. To make classification more effective, you move these e-mails to other folders and delete the empty ones.

You would like to read the e-mail that Mark sent last week. You remember it had an attachment, so you put the following query: "from: Mark received: last week hasattachment: yes"

There is an e-mail in your inbox containing company links that will be useful in the future, so you move it to some "universal" folder. At the same time you disable any potential auto-archiving of this folder to have all these universal e-mails available with one click.

There are some personal messages exchanged between you and your colleagues in your inbox, so you create a "personal" folder and move all these messages there.

You remember an e-mail discussion among your team about new technology. You remember it had three words in it: "new" "technology" and "presentation" but you are unsure about any other details. You put "new AND technology AND presentation" into the search bar and the e-mail is found.

Summary

The key to effective e-mail storage is to have just enough sub-folders in your inbox, so that similar messages are grouped together, but at the same time classification of new messages is quick and intuitive. On the other hand, our productivity at work is based on effective access to information. Learning how to translate our questions into proper search criteria is crucial. Remember that you will be doing this hundreds or thousands of times per year!

The first habit is all about classification: take action and determine if the material is garbage or suitable for future reference.

The second habit lets you store and access your materials effectively through quick categorization and efficient searches.

THE KEY TO EFFECTIVE E-MAIL STORAGE IS TO HAVE JUST
ENOUGH SUB-FOLDERS IN YOUR INBOX, SO THAT SIMILAR
MESSAGES ARE GROUPED TOGETHER, BUT AT THE SAME
TIME CLASSIFICATION OF NEW MESSAGES IS QUICK AND
INTUITIVE

Habit 3: Awaiting response

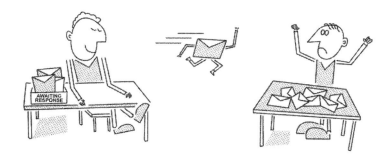

How many times have you sent an e-mail that asks for some action or information and you never received a response? We can blame others, but we need to take responsibility for completing what we began. The third habit will help you to complete and track all of your tasks, even if delegated.

Let us think for a minute about the sequence of actions that happen when you delegate a task to someone. You create a message, put all the required information there, and send it. Now it is among thousands of e-mails in your 'Sent' folder. You should apply a similar approach to these messages as in the first habit – these are messages that require an action, this time not from you, but from someone else.

Go to your inbox and create one additional folder that you can call 'Awaiting' or something similar. You can put a special sign such as '@' in front of its name, so that it appears first among all the folders. Now for every message that you expect a response or action, go to your 'Sent' folder and move such messages into your 'Awaiting' folder. It is very simple, because recently sent e-mail will appear first from the top if sorted by date. After you do that, you can easily take a daily or weekly look at the list of e-mails contained in your new folder, and send a gentle reminder for the lost ones when the time is appropriate.

The third habit consists of two parts: for every sent message, consider if a response is required and if so, move it to the right folder. Secondly, you must periodically check this folder. If you haven't received a response, send a reminder notice, and if you have, move it back to the "sent" folder.

If there is any specific deadline for a response you can put the reminder in your calendar and attach the message to it. This way you will be guarded twice.

FOR EVERY SENT MESSAGE, CONSIDER IF A RESPONSE IS REQUIRED AND IF SO, MOVE IT TO THE RIGHT FOLDER. PERIODICALLY CHECK THIS FOLDER. IF YOU HAVEN'T RECEIVED A RESPONSE, SEND A REMINDER NOTICE, AND IF YOU HAVE, MOVE IT BACK TO THE "SENT" FOLDER

Examples

You are writing an e-mail to your colleague asking him to send you his presentation from last week. Just after sending the e-mail, you move it from the "Sent" folder to "Awaiting". You also mark the message as "unread" to emphasize there is something in the folder.

There is an e-mail conversation that seems to have no end and you really need an answer. You add the biggest expert in that area to the e-mail thread asking him for help. After the e-mail was sent, you move it from the "Sent" to "Awaiting" folder.

The next morning, before starting your work, you scan your "Awaiting" folder and find three messages. The presentation you asked for was already received, so you move the e-mail back to "Sent." It is critical that today you receive an anticipated response, so you reply to the message once again and emphasize that a response is required today. The third message can wait, so you simply leave it in the folder.

Summary

Usually people hate delegating, simply because they are unable to easily track the progress. You may remember that you have sent two or three messages and are awaiting a response. What about five, ten, or twenty?

With a special folder and a simple habit, all the messages that are awaiting a response or action will be stored in one place, making it very hard to lose them.

Habit 4: Prioritization and Total Focus

Prioritization

The first three habits let you quickly categorize your e-mails, store and access materials effectively, and easily keep track of all the messages that require an action from someone else. As mentioned in the introduction, it may take two months of daily repetition before they become habits.

If you applied all the techniques correctly, your inbox is now a task list. It can be completely empty, but it usually contains several messages that are long and may take time to read and ponder, or require some other action. Messages that are likely to require an action from you are possibly marked with a different color or font.

E-mail clients can usually sort incoming messages by date, subject or sender, but it can be difficult to prioritize these messages. Whenever you feel that you are losing control of the priorities, you should immediately add the task to your mind map.

Total focus

Two questions will help you with the formation of the fourth habit: "Is it possible to complete this task in 3 minutes?" and "Is it possible to work for the next 25 minutes without distractions?" Three minutes in the first question could really be two or five, but the main point is to determine if you can complete the task quickly. The second question is about total engagement. Are you able to stop looking at your e-mails, communicators, SMS, and focus completely on your tasks for a limited amount of time? When you connect these two questions and only select "quick wins" from your inbox, you should be able to process most of it in less than half an hour and leave only longer tasks for the future. After completing this task, there shouldn't be more than a few e-mails left.

We will refer to this simple technique of cutting off distractions and interruptions for a limited amount of time, as the Pomodoro Technique. There are several tools available on your PC, tablet, and phone to help you with this. It can even be as simple as the old, analog alarm clock. Set the countdown to 25 minutes, stop all activity other than your current tasks, ask others to come later for non-critical issues, and focus completely until you hear the alarm signal. After your session is finished, take a break, refresh yourself, and take a short walk. Try one Pomodoro session a day and if you find it successful, add more.

Managers usually find it hard to organize at least one session per day, because they can't believe the world can exist without answering all calls and reading and answering all incoming e-mails on-the-fly. The key point is to understand the difference between critical, important activities (value judgment) and urgent activities (timing judgment). The truth is if this is not "critical and urgent," it may wait, but if you don't deal with your important tasks effectively, they will all soon become "critical and urgent." This is the trap that too many people fall into. If you have a desktop alert for all incoming messages disable it during the Pomodoro session - it is only distracting you! It will take at most 25 minutes before you read all messages. When you deal with the important issues in a timely manner, you realize that the number of critical and urgent tasks radically drops.

IF IT IS NOT "CRITICAL AND URGENT," IT MAY WAIT, BUT IF YOU DON'T DEAL WITH YOUR IMPORTANT TASKS EFFECTIVELY, THEY WILL ALL SOON BECOME "CRITICAL AND URGENT"

What your inbox is trying to tell you

Imagine that for a week you have been working according to the four habits mentioned above. After a few days one look at your Inbox will tell you the truth. Are there old messages that you are constantly avoiding? Do you feel you are able to process it all, given the speed they are received? Are most of the tasks coming from just one person? Observe it with a fresh mind and record the first feeling. It is important to remember that your brain is not a CPU, but also has emotions.

Be honest with yourself and think how you could improve the situation. Delegating tasks is not that hard, especially when you see that specific tasks drain your energy more than others. Telling someone that they put too much onto your shoulders may be hard. However, you may find that others respect responsible people who know their capacity and limitations.

Your inbox is always trying to tell you something. Never wait until "something happens," but each week take a small step forward based on your first impressions.

Examples

You have seven messages in your inbox. A quick look reveals that five of them should take no more than five minutes to answer, one requires thinking about the solution, and the last one will probably take you half an hour. There is nothing critical happening, so you turn off all the messengers, desktop alerts, mute your phone, and set the countdown timer to twenty-five minutes. You answer five quick e-mails one by one and immediately move them to the appropriate folder. Now you are left with just two longer messages. There are ten minutes left in your Pomodoro session, so you read the next message thoroughly and realize that the solution is pretty simple, so you answer the email with a short summary and move the message to the right folder. When you start thinking about the last message your alarm rings and it is time to lock your computer, take a short walk around the office, and have a few thoughts about your family and friends.

When you look at your phone, you realize that there is one missed call and one text message waiting for you. Your friend called and the message says he wants to see you this evening. Your calendar is free, so you create a new event and call him back to say that it would be really nice to see him again!

After coming back to your desk, you see that there are two people that wanted to talk to you over internal messenger (IM) and there are three new e-mails waiting. It takes one minute to categorize all your new e-mails and none of them requires your action, so your mailbox is left with just one message. You look at the conversations started and one of them seems to be longer and the person is in your office. Instead of typing the response and wasting your time, you go directly to her and a two-minute conversation solves the problem at hand. The last conversation turns out to concern a simple question.

You are involved in several conversations over IM at the same time. Two of them are longer, the rest seem short. You ask the two to wait for a few minutes and answer all the short questions one by one. For the remaining two, you ask the second one to wait for a couple more minutes, and ask the first if you could call directly. What could be a twenty-minute chat is now a five-minute phone call that you end with a smile and immediately ask the other person for another call.

You are in the middle of your Pomodoro session and someone comes to you in person asking for help. This is not critical, so you ask him for fifteen minutes, put a reminder in your calendar and immediately go back to your tasks. A bit later when you are fully focused on your current task, another person comes. This time it is critical, so you save your work and immediately address the problem. You feel you need to talk to this person one on one and it is about lunch time, so you invite him for lunch, where you freely elaborate on the problem.

You come back after lunch and realize that you have just received twenty new e-mails and most of them require your action. Now there are thirty-five messages in total waiting in your inbox. Fifteen seem to be very quick, so you respond one by one and leave twenty. It would take two days to address all of them, but you see that there are four main categories of action. You delegate two of them to your team members, forwarding all the required information in one message and then move the sent messages to your 'Awaiting' folder. Afterwards, you meet with them in person, give instructions, and answer all questions.   You then schedule one Pomodoro session and twenty-five minutes is enough to answer five e-mails, leaving you with five for a later time and two delegated tasks.

Summary

The fourth habit is all about priorities and focusing on the current task as much as possible. When you turn off your distractors, ask people for some time to yourself, delegate, and effectively use your task list and calendar, you are able to fully engage in your current task. When you focus on important tasks, the number of critical and urgent issues decreases.

Mastering your Calendar

Habit 5: The golden rule of your calendar

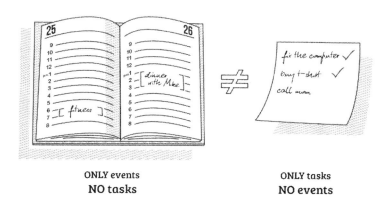

ONLY events
NO tasks

ONLY tasks
NO events

Take a minute to open your calendar. Let us take a close look at it, whether it is in electronic or paper form. There are two very important questions that inform the fifth habit – "Is this event bound to a specific time?" and "Is there any event I need to remember that I did not put in my calendar?" We can anticipate that you will form the fifth habit when you answer these two questions unconsciously and quickly.

An effective use of your calendar will relieve anxiety by allowing you to engage in your current task without looking at your watch and worrying about missing some important future event. The right tools will help you achieve this peace of mind.

Two of the most common mistakes of calendar usage involve using either too many or too few entries. Your calendar contains "too many" entries when you put your tasks as events and "too few" when you have to remember about events. A task is an action with an optional deadline. An event is something that will happen at a specific time whether or not you attend. The place for tasks is in your task list. The place for events is in your calendar. Never mix your task list with your calendar as they have completely different purposes.

Events that you create are usually meetings (it will be held, regardless if you attend) or reminders (something that will or should happen at specific time). If something can be done at different times, it's a task, not an event.

If you have to remember about something and did not create an event for it in your calendar, you may become distracted from focusing completely on your current task or you may forget about it all together.

Currently our smartphones and tablets integrate with e-mail accounts and calendars very well. In the past you had to make paper-based notes and use an alarm. Currently your device will ring and remind you about an event, helping you focus on the task at hand without missing any important events.

THE PLACE FOR TASKS IS ON YOUR TASK LIST.
THE PLACE FOR EVENTS IS IN YOUR CALENDAR.
NEVER MIX YOUR TASK LIST WITH YOUR CALENDAR AS
THEY HAVE COMPLETELY DIFFERENT PURPOSES

Examples

You want to meet with your team to discuss the latest findings, so you create an appointment, add mandatory and optional participants, possibly book a room as a resource, and put all the necessary information in the request. A reminder should be set to a few minutes beforehand if people are available on short notice, or hours or days if they need more time to get to the meeting place.

There is a company survey with a deadline set for the last day of the month. Because you don't want to do it right now, but don't want to miss the opportunity, you create an event for the date with a reminder set to a day or a week in advance.

For some reason, you want to track the mileage of your car on a weekly basis. Sunday evening seems like a good time, because usually there is no rush and you are likely to be close to the car. You create an event for Sunday evening and set the recurrence to weekly. The event can last 5 minutes, but with the reminder in place, you will strengthen your memory and after a few months, it will become a habit. Recording mileage is itself a task; however, since you want to repeat it on a weekly basis in a similar timeframe, it should be recorded as an event.

You would like to form a daily routine for the start of each workday. You consider planning your lunch in advance, writing down tasks that are critical for today, sending a snapshot of progress to your manager, and reading one article from one of your favorite online magazines. You create an event that will happen every work day at 8:30 AM, when you usually enter the office. The points mentioned earlier are put in the reminder, including the link to the magazine.

Summary

Your calendar and task list have different purposes and it is crucial not to mix them. The fifth habit addresses the distinction between a task and an event and provides you with the confidence to stay focused on your work without dealing with the stress of forgetting something important. When used wisely, your calendar will help you form other habits quickly and effectively.

Effective Task List

Habit 6: Task List - Mind Map

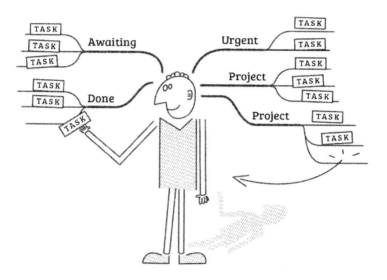

In the first five habits we addressed e-mail and calendar usage. A task list is the one remaining item to complete the big picture.

You probably already have a task list in one of the popular forms - a hand-written scrap on a sheet of paper, a simple text file, sticky notes, or a piece of software like "Remember The Milk."

All the techniques mentioned above work fine. However, for a long time I searched for a visually appealing task list that allows for easy prioritization, displays relation of tasks to bigger projects, shows delegated tasks, and works on any PC, Mac, or tablet.

I wanted to use a system that with one look would tell me where I was and signify the most important step forward. In the next chapters we will discuss the sixth habit - mind map - which will incorporate all such information.

Software required

To start, all you need is a mind mapping application. You can try several options available on your PC, Mac, or tablet and choose the one that suits you best.

Personally, I use FreeMind.

Mind map structure

Please run your application now and let us start. Suggested names for the root include: your first name, your job title, or simply "To Do" or "Tasks." Next, we can proceed with creating child nodes.

The right-hand side of the mind map will contain tasks to be completed by you, while the left-hand side will contain tasks that are already finished or are to be completed by others.

Your tasks are contained within projects or categories and are sorted by priority, with the most important ones on the top. A special category that should be your number-one priority is labeled "Urgent and Important." Tasks contained here are usually expected to be completed in the first time slot possible (minutes, hours). At the bottom there should be a category labeled "Important" that contains other important, uncategorized tasks. (Personally I hate the label "others" and much prefer "important." If it's not important, why bother?)

Let us begin with a very simple mind map structure that we will extend in the next few chapters.

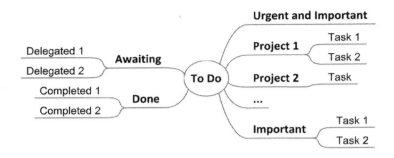

Basic mind map operation

The basic process for mind map operation is very straightforward – the ultimate goal is to move the tasks from the right-hand side to the left-hand side of the map and periodically perform its cleansing and prioritization:

1. Pick the next important task from the right-hand side

2. Perform the task and move it to "Done"
   or

3. Delegate to others and move it to "Awaiting"

These actions could be performed in a Pomodoro-like manner described in the chapter "Total Focus." Periodic cleansing and prioritization will be described with the seventh habit.

Since all the tasks and projects are prioritized, you should be able to simply scan the top tasks in each of the projects and focus first upon the "Urgent and Important" category if it is not empty.

Mind map is a visual representation that with one look should immediately reveal hidden information to you. Some projects will have many tasks, while others will be nearly empty. For example, this could mean that one of the projects is overloaded or actions for a project are unclear. You may also realize that your "Urgent and Important" category is never empty.

We will look into that a bit more in "What your mind map is trying to tell you" section.

THE ULTIMATE GOAL IS TO MOVE THE TASKS FROM THE RIGHT-HAND SIDE TO THE LEFT-HAND SIDE OF THE MAP AND PERIODICALLY PERFORM ITS CLEANSING AND PRIORITIZATION.

Building the right-hand part

Let us first focus on the right-hand part that contains your projects and categories filled with specific tasks.

First, tasks and project names are usually quickly discovered, while the rest will be filled in over time. Don't try to be too perfect at the first moment, just come up with something good enough to start with.

Let us work with the example of a person managing the office in an IT organization. The most important categories for daily work include office supplies, the building, travel assistance, and communication. A computer upgrade is coming, for which there will surely be a few related tasks.

This is how an initial mind map could look like in this case:

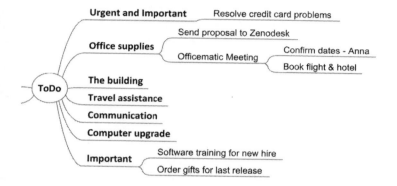

A helpful quality of a map is that tasks can be nested multiple times, as seen in the example above where "Officematic Meeting" is nested with the "Office supplies" category.

During the course of your week, whenever a task comes to mind, simply put it in your mind map. After a week the map should be fairly complete and may look similar to the one below:

THE MOST IMPORTANT PROJECTS AND TASKS
SHOULD BE CLOSEST TO THE TOP

Connection with inbox

You probably realize that we now have two task lists: your e-mail inbox formed with the first four habits and the mind map. Aren't they conflicting with each other?

E-mails that take longer to complete should be entered into the mind map as a task. Simply put, if the e-mail requires a quick response or action, it should be immediately completed, however if it takes more time, a task should be created. This allows easy prioritization and tracking of all the actions that need to be performed.

Examples of e-mails as tasks in the mind map displayed above include, "send feedback to Thomas," "send proposal to Zenodesk," or "analyze April statistics." An e-mail asking for some action was received and a response will take some time, which is why the task was created.

E-MAILS THAT TAKE LONGER TO COMPLETE SHOULD HAVE A CORRESPONDING TASK IN THE MIND MAP

Picking the next task

When it comes to picking the next task to perform, there is no clear procedure of what to do. Your mood, priorities, energy level, and context are changing all the time. You are not a machine and the rule of drawing the next action is fairly simple: given your priorities choose the one that will provide you the most fun and progress at the same time.

Projects, as well as their corresponding tasks, are sorted by priority. With just one look, you can scan the most important tasks and make an appropriate choice. In a multitasking environment it is crucial to have control over all projects at the same time and with just one look you should be able to notice which projects are going well and which require more attention.

Avoid putting too many tasks in the "Urgent and Important" category, because it reveals a dysfunction. For most of the time, this category should be empty and you should be able to focus on your important projects, rather than urgent issues.

YOU ARE NOT A MACHINE AND THE RULE OF DRAWING THE NEXT ACTION IS FAIRLY SIMPLE: GIVEN YOUR PRIORITIES CHOOSE THE ONE THAT WILL PROVIDE YOU THE MOST FUN AND PROGRESS AT THE SAME TIME

Managing projects

Your task list and projects are like a living organism. Along with their priorities they constantly change. The main purpose of having them all in the mind map is to keep them organized outside of your head.

Whenever you feel your map is not reflecting reality, you must make corrections. Please don't say "later!" There may be a new task or set of tasks that you are thinking about and they should immediately be written down and assigned a priority. If you relieve your memory, you will be able to focus completely on your current task without fearing that something will be lost.

Stagnancy is the biggest problem to avoid with your tasks and projects. The right-hand side of your map should be in a constant process of change. If you see that something looks exactly the same for a long time, it is time to address the issue. Maybe it is time to re-think the whole idea, get a clear picture of what needs to be achieved, or delegate some tasks and focus more on other projects?

There is also the trap of perfection, when you over-eagerly write down every possible task and the list no longer fits on your screen. There should be at least two or three tasks in each of your main projects to clarify your next steps, but not more than thirty in total.

WHENEVER YOU FEEL YOUR MAP IS NOT REFLECTING REALITY, YOU MUST MAKE CORRECTIONS. PLEASE DON'T SAY "LATER!"

Managing delegated tasks

Some of the tasks were delegated to others and you have clear evidence recorded in your mind map. You should periodically review that list and take an action: move to "Done" category, send a reminder, or assign the task to another person (including you).

This review can be performed once a day or once a week, depending on the urgency, but in most cases doing this every day before you leave the office is recommended.

When the task is finished, simply move it from "Awaiting" to "Done." If you are the person to continue the task, you can drag it back to the right-hand side. The key point is to make sure everything is progressing and nothing is lost, whether your responsibility or someone else's.

What your mind map is trying to tell you

If you try using your mind map in the manner described above, after a week you should be able to perform a simple exercise. Take just one look and try to sense where you are. There is so much information you can gain from it!

You can see how many tasks are in the "Done" and "Awaiting" categories and how many inhabit the right-hand side, noting the proportions. If you completed six tasks during the week, but you have thirty more in total, it means working like this will take you five weeks to complete all tasks, not including new, incoming ones (which always arrive!). It may force you to think about delegating some tasks the following week, especially if you see that your "Awaiting" category is nearly empty. You may also realize that you are simply incapable of completing so many activities at the same time.

A second or third review could also reveal tasks which were not completed or even not considered for the past few weeks. This is a clear signal to address the problem. Are they so boring? Or unimportant? Or maybe you don't have the right skills? It is the right time to address these issues!

Your mind map is also showing you how your projects are progressing. Just take a look at their sizes and how they changed over the course of the week and what is actually in the "Done" category. On a weekly basis you should be able to perform such analysis and cleanup the "Done" category.

Examples

You look at your task list and realize that the top task is in the "Urgent and Important" category and involves fixing your credit card problems. It seems that this requires a call to the bank and you are in the right mood to do it, so you open their website, call them, tell them about the problem, and it gets immediately fixed. This task is moved to the "Done" category.

Your "Urgent and Important" list is empty and you realize that organizing a meeting with the new international supplier is the timely thing to do. There is a task to confirm dates with Anna, you see she is available on chat and she says she is free to talk. You go to her office to talk to her. The date of the trip is agreed upon and while thinking about the trip you pass by an IT room, which reminds you to ask for AC adaptors. You get two and come back to your desk. "Confirm dates – Anna" and "Get AC adaptors" are moved to the "Done" category.

Your next task is discussing continuous problems with Section D air conditioning. There are four people that need to be involved in the discussion, so you schedule a meeting, which involves booking a room, writing the agenda, and sending invites. Another task is moved to the "Done" category; however, it will only be fully completed after the meeting is done.

Another task is "Analyze April statistics." There is a person in your team that enjoys doing this and she is free, so you ask her to do it and move the task into the "Awaiting" category.

There is an e-mail in your inbox that asks for an analysis of statistics before next Friday. You create a calendar event for next Friday, attach the e-mail and set a reminder to two days beforehand, then move the e-mail into the "Awaiting" folder in your inbox.

The reminder pops up a few days later and you realize the task has still not been completed by your teammate. You immediately ask her if she is on schedule to complete this, and it turns out that it just needs polishing. You review the document and it is good enough. You reply to the e-mail contained in your "Awaiting" folder, attach the presentation, move the e-mail to the proper folder, and move the task from the "Awaiting" to the "Done" category.

You notice increasing problem with the hard disk and overall performance of your computer. It may affect your work in the coming days, so you move the whole "Computer upgrade" project to the top of your project list, just below "Urgent and Important." Next, you immediately sit down and prepare the list of critical software and at the end move the task to the "Done" category.

Summary

The sixth habit is the heart of the system described in this book. It is visual, quick to learn, and allows for easy prioritization, categorization, and tracking. Consequently, it should engage both hemispheres of your brain.

In my experience, I have had people learn this during a one-hour session, and within a few days enthusiastically report that finally they could see the structure and the progress of their tasks. At the same time, they mentioned that it was easy to track the tasks delegated to others.

Cleansing

Habit 7: Weekly cleanup and daily startup

There is one last habit to form and it is all about sustainability. Have you ever tried to organize something, filled with an initial burst of energy? The sky is bright, you are energetic, changes seem clear, and there is plenty of good energy. However, within a few weeks or months these days may feel far away.

The thing we desperately need is a constant "inspect and adapt" cycle. You have to constantly monitor yourself and act when necessary.

Managing your tasks and projects should take as little time as possible while giving you a clear picture of your priorities, goals, and upcoming responsibilities. It is crucial that this "system" is healthy over long periods, not only initial weeks or months.

MANAGING YOUR TASKS AND PROJECTS SHOULD TAKE AS LITTLE TIME AS POSSIBLE WHILE GIVING YOU A CLEAR PICTURE OF PRIORITIES, GOALS, AND UPCOMING RESPONSIBILITIES. IT IS CRUCIAL THAT THIS "SYSTEM" IS HEALTHY OVER LONG PERIODS, NOT ONLY INITIAL WEEKS OR MONTHS

Weekly cleanup

Once every week, preferably on the last workday of the week, you should do a small summary. Put a recurring event in your calendar for at least half an hour on that day. For a typical office it could be Friday at 2 or 3 PM. Go ahead and put a plan in the event message:

1. Clean up completed tasks

2. Send reminders for "Awaiting" tasks

3. Re-prioritize

4. Think about next week and next month

When the reminder pops up, do yourself a favor: mute your phone and turn off all messengers. You could have done a really good job over the week, but it is crucial that you completely focus yourself during this summary. The task requires your thoughts, feelings, and total engagement. You are in a long-distance run and it is time to look around!

First task: delete all tasks in the "Done" category, but first take a look at the list. Usually you do not remember all of them and it is a surprise how much you accomplished in just a few days. What are your feelings when you see that list? Are you proud or are you feeling drained of your energy? This is very important input when we address task number four.

Second task: scan through tasks in the "Awaiting" category and ensure that they are on track or delete them if already completed. After your summary is completed you may need to send a reminder via e-mail or take a short walk through the office to see the people responsible for the tasks.

Third task: Look at the priority of your projects and the tasks nested within each project. Are they correct? Does your map really reflect reality? Is there anything new or more important? Is a critical task missing? When you complete this point, ensure that the map accurately reflects what is going on in your projects.

Fourth task: Now open your calendar to the following week, then look at the task list and think about the next few days. The last few days could have been a real mess, but that is the past. What potential improvements could you implement next week? Sometimes subtle changes make a huge difference and allow you to feel as if you control reality, not the opposite. When you are finished, take a short flight – look at your life from the perspective of a few hundred meters.

What about your relationships? Work-life balance? Are you still having fun? Do you feel you are developing? Is your vision clear? You could set the countdown timer to 15 minutes and consider these questions for a moment. Sometimes there is a point to be added to the agenda of the next meeting with your boss to talk about your professional development. You may consider taking a course to improve your communication skills or change your working hours to spend more time with your kids. At the end, it is important that you feel as if you did a good job the past week and more productivity is ahead in the coming week.

WHAT ABOUT YOUR RELATIONSHIPS?
WORK-LIFE BALANCE?
ARE YOU STILL HAVING FUN?
DO YOU FEEL YOU ARE DEVELOPING?
IS YOUR VISION CLEAR?

What usually happens is that people avoid reflecting upon their work while in the office, thinking that they will do it at home. However, immediately after leaving the office many focus on their private life and do not revisit this topic. Consequently, this simple, life-giving activity can be pushed from one week to another and remain incomplete. Usually we find time for such reflection when situations spin out of control. Do yourself a favor and clean your house regularly.

The four points mentioned as "weekly cleanup" reminders could also be easily extended to include ones of your own. For example, you may need to send weekly reports to your boss each week. In this case, point number five could be "Ensure weekly report was sent." When you leave your office for the weekend, you should feel that you closed the chapter of your previous week and you are ready to begin a new one.

Daily startup

With all the techniques mentioned above, you should be able to form a healthy "system" in just a few weeks. There is one more improvement you can make that I found useful in many situations.

When we begin work, it usually takes some time to get into the daily routine. Sometimes it takes longer than expected and sometimes it is hard to get started in the first place!

As humans, we need structure and some kind of routine or ritual to help us to put our thoughts in order. A reminder that pops up every morning, just after arriving to the office, helps to organize the whole day. Put a few actions in the reminder and no matter your emotional state or what happened before work, you have a routine to help you start the day. Create a recurring meeting for every work day, the earlier the better.

Initially at least three points are required: look at the calendar and events for the day, categorize your e-mails (habits one to four) and scan through "Awaiting" tasks to check if anything is becoming critical.

Your events for today will create the background - you can't move them. The space between them will be filled with tasks, possibly providing you the most progress and fun at the same time. Tasks delegated to others can block you completely, so it is important to monitor them and react as quickly as possible.

Other tasks may involve looking through various metrics, statistics, project progress reports, or company news. You may also spend time reading something meaningful (time limited!), planning your lunch, and sending a snapshot of your progress to the manager.

Examples

You had a terrible morning at home, you can barely remember how you got to the office, you start looking at random pages and feel overwhelmed by the number of tasks to achieve. Suddenly your "daily startup" reminder pops up and you follow the list of tasks one by one: the calendar shows two meetings spaced by an hour, which looks like a potential lunch break - you will really need good company for today! It seems that your tasks will be concentrated in the morning and then two hours after lunch. You feel your morning could be devoted to one group of tasks including the urgent ones and in the afternoon you could progress onto the second project. You stand up and go to your colleague to close the first urgent task and when you come back to your desk, you feel your day has already started and your thoughts are back on the right track.

It is Friday afternoon - the time to do your weekly summary. You realize that eleven tasks were done this week and all the projects are progressing fine, so you smile, because it seems like a productive pace! There are twenty tasks on your right-hand side – a healthy amount. There are three tasks in the "Awaiting" category, so after the summary you go around the office and ask different people about the status of the tasks and relax a bit at the same time.

When you think about your last week you remember that you lost a few hours because a server was down and you recall such a disruption happening every month. You talk to your colleagues and they have had similar experiences. Fixing this problem could be a new task or project – you will likely write an e-mail to the IT department and put it into your awaiting queue. Maybe they are just not aware that it is causing so much trouble for others?

While looking at the balance of your projects, you realize you have progressed well on each of them and there is nothing urgent, but you notice that "Order flowers for section C" has been there for quite a long time. After a moment you realize that it is unclear what is actually expected of that task, so you put it on the agenda of your next meeting with your boss.

Summary

No matter how great the productivity system you try to put into practice, the key point, really, is sustainability.

If it is not working over the period of several months or even years, why should you bother starting it at all?

No system is perfect if it is not "yours." Even subtle changes that you introduce after each weekly summary can develop into something bigger and after several months you can really feel that it is all yours — some of the habits we formed were only the beginning, a starting point. After some time of adapting the system to your responsibilities and working style you won't be able to simply copy it for others to use. It will be uniquely yours.

The seventh habit is all about concluding the work week "sprint," so that you feel closure on one chapter of your life and are ready to begin new challenges. Each week is like a run — you should be able to achieve your goals with maximum speed and then stop, take a rest, and be ready to start a new run. This is why goals and priorities have to be clear and all the habits in place — only when you clearly see the finish line and your muscles work unconsciously, can you run with maximum speed and enjoyment.

The feeling when you cross the finish line is worth it.

No matter how great the productivity system you try to put into practice, the key point, really, is sustainability. If it is not working over the period of several months or even years, why should you bother starting it at all?

The First Step

If you got to this point and did not try to put any of these habits into practice, this is the time when you really should. Gathering useful information will not help you, only practical and positive responses will create change. Go ahead and act!

If you don't know how to start, turn off all your distractors, focus for the next half an hour and try to go through the list below — do not spend more than five minutes on any point and if you have problems with the time limit, use an alarm clock:

☐ Download and print A4 (or letter) handout from www.effectivemultitasking.com and put it on your desk or on the wall near the place where you sit.

☐ Go to your e-mail client and clarify your folders — there should be a maximum of seven to ten folders. If there are already existing ones, try to group similar ones together.

☐ Classify the first twenty e-mails in your inbox according to the first habit: does it requires an action from me OR is it material for future reference OR is it garbage?

☐ Fill your calendar with events that you need to actively remember — meetings, deadlines, reminders.

☐ Download and open your Mind Mapping software, create the basic structure (described in the sixth habit) and write five to ten tasks that initially come to mind. If you have a problem with choosing the perfect software, start with FreeMind.

☐ Create a daily startup reminder that will help you form the habits.

☐ Think about which habit will potentially give you the most progress and make a point to start with it! Remember that forming the habit will take you two months of daily repetition!

     o Read the chapter for that habit, write down the key points so that you see them many times a day, and put them into practice.

     o Make a commitment to try it every day for the next 30 days and focus during your daily startup activities.

Results will come when you start forming your habits!

Read more

I was strongly influenced by many books and articles and I would like to list some of the ones I found worth studying:

- "The Seven Habits of Highly Effective People" by Stephen R. Covey – great book to read on character and long-term changes in your life.
- "Getting Things Done" by David Allen – a complete "system" that will help you understand how much information we keep in our heads and how it is lost there.
- "Zen To Done" by Leo Babauta – a simpler, practical response to "Getting Things Done," based on habits.
- http://www.pomodorotechnique.com – the technique of "total focus" that will help you be more productive. Includes related software, hints and materials.
- "Flow: The Psychology of Optimal Experience" by Mihaly Csikszentmihalyi – great book about what inspires us and what really keeps us engaged in our tasks.
- "Man's Search For Meaning" by Viktor E. Frankl – not only about being effective, this book addresses the broader issues of what we fill our lives with.

Thank you for buying my book!

I wish you all the best on your adventure to organize yourself and unleash your productivity and creativity.

For more information and materials visit us:

- http://www.effectivemultitasking.com
- http://facebook.com/effectivemultitasking

About the author

Piotr Nabielec is an IT trainer and coach who has worked in a number of different roles for small companies and several large corporations like Motorola, Nokia Siemens Networks, and Sabre Holdings.

Piotr, based in Krakow, Poland, is known for his passion helping people and companies become more productive. He currently contributes to Lifehack.org and writes a blog on Personal Productivity. As a conference speaker, Piotr usually talks about productivity, processes, and human factors in the IT world.

Visit: http://about.me/piotrnabielec

Printed in Great Britain
by Amazon